JUST
LIKE
THAT

with a billion best wishes
Jervis Ireland

Other poetry by Kevin Ireland

JUST LIKE THAT

KEVIN IRELAND
NEW POEMS

Quentin Wilson
PUBLISHING

to Janet

First published 2021 by
Quentin Wilson Publishing
105 Moncks Spur Road
Christchurch 8081
New Zealand
wilson.quentin@gmail.com
www.quentinwilsonpublishing.com

ISBN 978-0-9951437-3-9 (print)

A catalogue record for this book is available from the
National Library of New Zealand

Front cover photo: Ida Kar
'Kevin Ireland, 1959', National Portrait Gallery, London

Back cover photo: Photographer unknown

With thanks to Christine Roberts & Roger Steele
for expert editorial assistance

Cover and page design:
Quentin Wilson Publishing
Copyright © 2021 Quentin Wilson Publishing

Printed in Aotearoa New Zealand by YourBooks,
Wellington

Contents

I:

POEMS FOR PANDEMICS

On the other hand …

From time to time an agent, coded influence or bug
jumps from one host to another and a common consequence
of this is the prospect of disaster, so you'd think
all modern humans would have learnt to be prepared,
at least enough to spare us from the joke that we have been
preoccupied with far more urgent matters.

Until quite recently we could blame such threats
on other-worldy interventions. Plagues existed in the air,
propelled by breezes, spooky smells or even casual glances.
Pandemics offer more than just a modern change of name,
for we've discovered how the real dirty work
gets done in unseen fluids, tissues, gases –

and we have proof of how the rules apply,
the likely risks we run and how the cost of saving money,
by not stacking up secure supplies and working out
effective plans, is totally excessive – and we have to
wonder why it took so long for many to decide
on effective lockdown, social distancing and isolation.

Yet perhaps this visitation will unite us and one day even
seem a useful force for good. Possibly we'll survive
the Delta strain with higher aspirations – though
it does come hard that millions suffer, old friends die
and some still snuffle for obstructive answers
in feeble nonsense and ludicrous conspiracies.

A brief journal of a pandemic

The first news of the outbreak
that we'd soon be calling a pandemic
suggested it would be just another pain
to faze your average hypochondriac.

After all, it had the decency to aim itself
at those who lived in distant lands
and bought their food in market stalls.
On top of which we heard it chose

its victims only from the old or ill
or critically decayed. Meeting up
with such a malady seemed far beyond
all likelihood – except that

I'd forgotten I was nearing 90
when I flew off absent-mindedly
to meet my wife in a foreign land
where immediately we discovered

it had turned into a madhouse
run by lunatics. With luck, we paid
the extra, bought new tickets and managed
to slip out again – and when we got

back home we blessed our government
for being calm, practical, dependable
and sane. And so far, both my wife
and I have managed to survive.

We get on with the daily work
we're used to, so our existences
are little changed. And up till now
we're eating well and we enjoy

an evening wine. It shakes us still that we
were met by craziness in once-reliable
locations where several of our friends
would soon be very sick or die,

yet the underlying horror of it all
remains the nonstop bluster
and the unrepentant lies, the evasions,
accusations, plus the smug refusal

to accept even the basic duties of high office
revealed by all the ambitious braggarts
and the pompous farts who went
to so much strutting trouble to gain

a show-off moment in the spotlight
of their times. It's true and perfectly
acceptable that human failures
in a drawn-out fight against a lethal virus

are all too likely on the way
to its containment and eventual defeat,
but to project a systematic uselessness
as the best path to eventual victory

requires an almost bonkers genius
in so many leaders of the world. I hold
a faith that we'll get over this – and all of us
will learn we have to share the blame.

Virus versus golf

Walking across the local golf course
early on today, it crossed my mind
in the idle way that simple words
can catch alight from cheerful thoughts
that it was now almost impossible
to be clocked by a misdirected ball
or carelessly swung club,

two dreadful prospects that have
always seemed good reason up till now
to keep away from golf – even though
I can believe that players seldom
kill each other and I'm well aware
the problem's partly mine for I've never
been instructed where to step

or when or where to stop. I delighted
in this stroll through fearsome greens,
only because the far worse menace
of a virus had put an end to play
and through a painless paradox
made a dodgy and unnerving
place of danger superlatively safe.

A room with more than a view

Let me describe the room in which I try to work.
It has a desk, a chair, a cupboard – and the walls
have shelves, photographs, notes, paintings
and cartoons. There are books and papers
strewn or stacked and tumbling everywhere.

For decades I have managed to avoid the oppression
of this mess by gazing through a window
at the far worse clutter of the view outside –
the shambles caused by tangled branches,
clouds, birds, falling leaves – and always

by the reckless carry-on of the weather.
But never had it crossed my mind that out there,
one day, I'd endure a baffling and alarming
and deliberate attack. Yet through the glass –
so I can now record – the world I looked on

has turned out to be enraged, malevolent
and treacherous. A virus stalked the shadows
in our gardens, skulked about the trees,
leapt from roof to roof and stole across back fences.
It slithered, unmasked, up the driveways

to our houses and puffed through all our keyholes.
I had to close the curtains for the first time ever
then firmly shut the door. I've had no option
but to shift the desk – and I've confronted
face-to-face at last, the chaos that is mine.

The elderly pandemic

There's not the slightest point in pussyfooting
round the problem any longer: the *other* epidemic –
the matter of the hordes of ancient human beings –

is far more dangerous than this pop-up little virus.
It's quite beyond control. The fact is that, until
the recent past, we could rely on wars, ignorance,

lack of medication, plus the routine visitation
of some catastrophe or pestilence, to put a limit
on the lifespans of us all (and especially

of our neighbours). Yet on the whole, and despite
the bad news every day, our chances of survival
are improving, and as I near 90

my doctor keeps a scientific eye on me
and makes whatever readjustments may be
necessary on occasion to keep the chemicals

that I'm entirely made of (and which
I'm used to calling *me*) in a kind of equilibrium
that may not rate as up-to-very-much

but gets me by in a patched yet mostly unalarming
working order. Of course, we keep on dying
in our millions, but we can put it off for so long

it's quite easy to forget it's taking place.
This is the *real* plague – the infestation and contagion
that ought to drive us to distraction. Decrepit,

senile mobs are spreading round the world
and it's now time to face the facts and find solutions
and take some drastic action. Meanwhile

my senior friends and I wrestle with the problem.
We hope to live a great deal longer and devote
a lot more time to coming up with answers.

Visit to a high-risk hotspot

In a far-off country where we stayed a little more than
just a year ago, the death toll of the virus began to rise
to several dozen, then a hundred, every horrifying day.
'Just keep calm,' the politicians prompted, 'and remember
there are tens of millions of us anyway – and all

through winter influenza knocks us off in even greater
numbers – so where's the sudden problem?'
I did not for a minute think this argument was
statistically persuasive or morally encouraging –
especially since it seemed to have an earnest link

to an unregenerate conviction that the calculated sacrifice
of legions of the elderly, the frail and failing
would prove to help the young, the virile and the jaunty
build up something terrifying that they presented
with a smile as perfect herd immunity. I had grown up

in times of worldwide war and misery in which
our side had only just prevailed against the maniacs
in fancy dress who spouted poisonous phrases
quite like that, so my wife and I escaped in haste –
and though I am aware that, as I write these words,

a stray, pernicious something may be heading headlong
straight towards us, I do have doubts that it will claim
to be an instrument of public policy. We've felt much more
secure since we've been home and – as we don't
take part in riots or rash escapades these days –

we spend lost hours looking busy, mixed in with real
bouts of work, as well as reading, scrawling, walking,
napping, cooking, talking. Vicious herds still stray
across some unconvincing headlines, but we believe
they never will be trusted – and keep our fingers crossed.

Talking yet again about this virus, sorry!

This jumped-up virus has behaved obnoxiously for such
a microscopic dot of near-nothingness, distracting
our attention from the majestic and momentous presence
of the stars, moons, planets and all the comets put together –

and, by the way, the sum of these vast bits and pieces
whizzing round about in all the known galaxies (and that's
not even adding in the hidden extras) adds up to far more
than the grains of sand on every beach in all the world.

Which means that when my friends and I discuss this virus
we tend to aim our comments at the anecdotal ends
of weird analogy rather than at systematic speculation.
We deal in quirky possibilities not entirely beyond belief

and droll associations that keep popping from our pasts –
studies that have also been most useful in exposing ways
we have collectively misspent our lives in spite of so much fun.
However, this poem is, sort of, half a plain apology –

for we have come up with no scrap of wisdom that could be
of help to anyone in a symposium on the problems that
this speck of frightful torment has been causing while we've been
staring at the sky and chattering. We have no science

that may help, no brilliant intuitions and not a tiny,
sparkling drop of inspiration. The things that poetry achieves
can't offer businesslike or hands-on help to those in need.
In fact, we ought to stop here at this very point and let

the experts hold the floor – we've found them brisk, courteous,
packed to the eyebrows with practical advice, and they are
crammed with goodwill for our species – maestros of integrity –
yet that's as far as I can go because it's where the stars

and moons, etcetera, do come in again – for it turns out
that we lie awake at night recalling lines of half-forgotten verse
and this presses us to postulate with awe (as we gaze
at the immensity of space and ponder on entailments

of infinity) whether poetry, like viruses, may also have
the brazen perkiness of pure invention, the impudence
of inexhaustible mutation. Our thoughts on tragedy and comedy
are mercurial – and change as fast as switching masks.

Rumours of the virus

Those of us who've had our heads down and devoted
patient months to warding off the frustrations of enforced
confinement in the space we share with partners,
relatives or friends – whom we were fortunate to have around

to join the phantoms, nightmares, shades we couldn't
lock outside – now face rumours that it's been a hoax
and we've experienced a secret test of public discipline
that will prove to be a governmental pretext to force

our mildest, sanest citizens to tame their teeming lives.
There's a dark, resentful muttering going on that we
shall soon get used to a restricted way of life in which
we'll never meet again except in well formed queues

with masks and antiseptic sprays and social distancing.
They mumble that we'll learn to hate the shameless waste
of tourist travel, loitering in parks, loafing in a library or café
and other frightful, costly means of idling and frivolity.

I'm always cheered by an opposition that finds it such
a happy pleasure to conspire against a fanciful conspiracy.
The thrill of knocking over windmills comes second only
to the fantasy of triumph over a dead certainty.

The mind and body problem solved

My superannuated body told me: Don't even
dream of going for a walk this morning. It complained
of rumpty joints, a sorry, sore and swollen toe,
a disconcerting seizure in the lower region

of the back, then added that it thought it could be
suffering an attack by – wait for it – a bat or
pangolin-transmitted virus. Yes, it used those
very words, then followed them with such

a grisly and convincing shudder that I almost
ran for cover (except my body couldn't).
Naturally, I definitely wasn't going to stand for
such grotesque malingering, so I marched it

down the road as fast as I could force it.
This overwhelming, painful, unexpected exercise
brought the apparatus to its collective senses
and it soon apologised for the extravagant excuse

it had so misapplied. I stopped and thanked my body
for its honesty, and said that if it liked we could
start the day again. It picked up snappily
and suggested that we ought to stroll back home

and celebrate. We did, and soon it helped me lift
my feet so I could stretch full length and fit them
over one arm of the sofa while my spine leant back
on cushions and I could raise a glass of wine.

Amazing how my parts and pieces were restored.
Not an ache or twinge – or virus – bothered me.
I can't recall when last I checked my various bits
and felt them ticking over even half so happily.

Rosy glory

It adds a risky feeling to the morning
when you check your latest slide towards collapse.
You've been attacked again at night by demolition experts
with a flair for comic artistry. They've worked you over
in your sleep – pounding, crumpling parts of you
into a battered wreck. And as a little extra
they've tied your thoughts in knots.

Luckily, you have enough experience to take
your time, with lots of steady breathing, before
you slowly verify the pigment and the disposition of the sky,
after which you have a go at bending unreliable joints
then stretching out your arms and legs to see
if there's the faintest chance they'll raise
your frame into a getting-up position.

From now on things cheer up a bit
and you make progress through the day. Vaguely,
you are on your way again. There's a heady magic in the air,
because you know some flighty, fickle matter is sure
to arise and push aside anxieties on how to cope
with painful processes that really may have
helped you crack on gainfully with work.

The rosy glory of achieving ripe old age
is that, exactly when you seem about to buckle
under all the strain of how to keep things going, there's an office
in your head where – just as you begin to topple – you may
redeem the situation by hanging out this warning:
'Mad and ancient patient locked in isolation.
Caution. Danger. Huge risk of contagion.'

2:

POEMS ON INSCRUTABILITIES, IRRELEVANCIES & INCONGRUITIES

Today's love poem

for Janet

Love poems sometimes blossom
from dishevelled gardens in the head.
One minute you're weaving down a street
walking into lampposts and the next

you're sitting in a coffee shop
jotting down a poem that flowered
from inside you on a matter even older
than the two of us – as we are constantly

reminded by official documents that have
no notion of reality. It's not the fact that love
and poetry can bloom like this,
the marvel is the way it seeds. Perhaps

it's carried on the wind – a warm one
with a scent of roses. This is my love poem
for today. It's written. Nothing else.
It wouldn't wish to offer explanations.

Times we won the race against Time

i.m. Mai Thai restaurant, closed 2020

Our lives are over in only half-a-jiffy,
yet Time will fool around with years in billions.
An age can pass while Time drags out a basic task of evolution,
yet we get flicked aside in fractions of an instant
and miss out on the riddles yet to come.

Most people find the way to slow down Time
is to stretch out in the sun upon a hill, then chew a straw
and revel in the view. Time loses concentration, begins to yawn,
mumbles slackly, then half-shuts both its heavy eyes.
But friends and I discovered, at the Mai Thai –

before the day it closed its doors forever –
a foolproof strategy to banjax Time entirely.
A midweek, lazy, laughing lunch, always with the best of friends,
a stack of fine food and several bottles of good wine,
would stop Time absolutely in its tracks.

Where did the paper-boys go?

My grandson dealt with this obscure question
by asking me to tell him more about these boys made out
of paper. Were they held together with Scotch tape
and string, or were they glued or stitched or stapled?
Did they flutter in the wind? It was beyond his
comprehension that little children, once upon a time,

would deliver newspapers on pushbikes all around
his neighbourhood – just as they would also mow
old ladies' lawns, thus saving resting fathers
from the chance discovery that trimming grass could ever
possibly become an adult chore. We young were at it
all the time, jamming papers into letterboxes and pushing

heavy mowers – for a pittance – past the flowers
and shrubs of gardens in the suburbs. Both tasks now
are occupations for grown-ups. Housewives in the streets
distribute papers, adverts, magazines, while men
in flash cars tow their gross and glinting trailers to disgorge
machines with petrol engines, turning kids' work

into lofty enterprises. I still whizz around my garden
with a mower, though I can't help recollecting how,
when young, I made a solemn declaration to myself
that I would never mow another lawn when I grew old.
And so perhaps my whole existence merely adds more proof
that real men can handle jobs as well as paper-boys.

One more fourteenth poem

Decades ago I understood I had the basis of a book
whenever I set out to write a fourteenth poem.

Double-sevens make a fortnight – and double-fortnights
make a lunar month – and this celestial harmony

of numbers signalled I was on my way. Plus, fourteen
has a unique link to sonnets and their matchless form,

even without a rhyme, as is the modern manner.
Fourteen's magic fascination hung absolutely

on the strength of pure suggestion, so it never failed
to fire me up as it led me to my desk, slapped paper down

in front of me and saw the job right through.
I resolved to scrawl a thirteenth poem only once.

Pencils vanished – ink ran dry – it took me months
to write another word. One shot was enough.

Slapstick comedy

All the structural bits of me –
every bone, joint, muscle, sinew,
organ, vessel, cavity, protrusion,
plus the skin that wraps them –
are not performing even half as well

as they used to in the good old days
when I rarely spared a second thought
upon the elemental, orderly
and practical mechanics that made
the human apparatus tick.

My whole attention was centred
on extravaganzas or delights
or on some passing curiosity, appetite
or whim. I relished all I ate and drank,
and loved the best of company.

Today once more I'm lunching
with old friends, but the talk no longer
dwells on tastes, pranks, passions
or our farcical ambitions. Instead,
we chat about a dicey, slippery world

where the streets are getting steeper
and stairs can multiply as we begin
to climb them, where distance is elastic
and can stretch out as our breath
gets shorter, and years may whistle by

and barely leave a trace. Yet we turn this
into jokes as we try to keep a grip –
though the ones that get the laughs
seem to end with slapstick punchlines
where we fall flat on our faces.

Time of the bedsitters

Who didn't spare a quiet, triumphant
grin of satisfaction as they climbed the social
scale and left behind the nosy trespassing
of overcrowded boarding houses and rented
one of the makeshift bedsits of the nation?

From that moment on we had a private key
to a single room that we could call our own.
Our cash paid for a bed, a chest of drawers,
a chair, a hook to hang a coat, a frail table,
a tiny place to cook, plus the marvel of a sink

and running water. We had to share a bath,
but a bedsit was a place where we could
lock out the whole world and think alone.
Bedsitters altered the condition of our lives
and though I wouldn't go so far as to suggest

that this in some way lent us trendiness or taste
it was most certainly a giant improvement.
And what it did promote was the priceless gift
of ingenuity in our domestic dispositions.
The point being that we now had every right

to come and go whenever we would wish –
to dip into a book or pour a glass, drift off to sleep,
and even have (or be) a visitor. Ah, that was it …
we were free to slip along the road at night
and tap on the window of a newest friend.

A grandfather in transports

i.m. Joseph McKenney

My maternal grandfather left New Zealand for Australia
in a sailing ship. He did consider going by steam
but asked: 'What if the engine stops?' Canvas looked
far more dependable. His opinion never changed.

When he returned to Wellington he saw a motorcar
and fell down laughing, for instantly he understood
it needed roads and bridges and could never beat a horse.
On top of which, you couldn't feed it hay and grass.

For those who wished to travel overland he insisted
there was only one invention to manifest the brilliance
and the far reach of the human mind –
the railway train, a machine that hurled itself

along twin iron rails, crossing our fair country
often at a scheduled time. And the wondrous virtue
it displayed above all else was that you knew the one
and only place in town it left from and arrived.

Yet the mode of transport that gave him most delight
was a polished pair of boots. In red bush-singlet
(buttoned to the neck), shiny suit with belted trousers,
ancient watch-and-chain, a bowler hat and heavy

hawthorn walking-stick, he'd set off to admire the land
and stop all passers-by with talk on poetry, religion,
politics. He had the magic gifts of memory and fluency,
and was completely and forever wrong – yet right.

How poems take us out to lunch

*With thanks to many dozens of wonderful lunch guests
(and the staff) at three main central restaurants over
more than three decades – and now at the Shakespeare Hotel.*

Good poems will greet you in the morning
with a crafty smile as they encourage you
to wear clean socks and always check
to pull them up from time to time each day.

And though you fully comprehend that every other
act of getting dressed is bound to set off twinges
in some sinew or a muscle that you'd
never thought to notice until now,

true poems acknowledge brave commitment
and they'll reward you with a slice of lemon
in your tea to add a snap to what their words
and lines are going to say. They'll also wish

to clear your mind with gentle exercise,
so they'll often walk you through a local park
and make you sit down while they stop to think.
They're never less than most agreeable

to neighbours and they'll greet all strangers
with a wink. Then every now and again
they'll lead you to a bus stop and they'll
take you into town, where they will always

guide you to a chair and offer you the joy
of meeting friends and eating lunch with chat
and laughs. The very best of poems will even
twist a bottle-cap and offer you a drink.

Poem for Roderick Finlayson

I have never attended
a Catholic funeral
half as jolly as Rod's.

Everyone had no doubt
that here before us lay
a sure bet for heaven.

I have never met a man
more deep in goodness,
free from any malice

and truly pure in heart.
I also think that he was
sometimes wrong – though

for the best of reasons.
People of ideals, decency
and innocence can heap

burdens on our minds.
Rod squared circles to the 39th
transcendental point

without a need to count
for he was one of neatest,
squarest dealers ever to have lived.

If he often troubled
our consciences he told us
how we had to live with it.

A solid gift that has no
counterfeits. He was a saintly,
smiling, loving man.

The one good reason for writing

It's a slow, relentless process, writing books,
and it tests your resolution. You produce
this tempting offering, with best-bright words,
mostly spelt correctly and with the grammar
nearly right, and it shines from splashy covers,

and you suggest a price that's well within
the limits of a modest budget, and then
what's next? Some lowlife misfit
thinks the time has come to patronise you.
Hard to believe, but that's the way it is.

Weirdos, crackpots, cranks will take
a condescending workout on your lines,
which only they can read the wrong way round
and upside-down. Amazing, but the truth is
it's a hard slog writing books, and it never

gives you rest. The only reason why I don't
give up is that it keeps me in at nights, which
means I save a pile of cash for treats to come
when I go out with friends and splash the lot –
on wine and love and riotous good times.

That and this

Titles of our poems could light a blazing fire across
the skies and entice us into states of stanza-hood,
which may perhaps reveal transcendence.
Yet generally they don't. As a possibility, I'd never

rule this out – remember how Belshazzar was alarmed
to read that writing on the wall – but this has not
transpired so often that you'd ever lay a bet on it.
There's always half a chance that we may read

a flaming message and that this will then illuminate
and change us all forever, though it seems more likely
that we'll spy a spark behind our eyes that lights
a shadow in the dark. *That to this* is, usually,

the way this has to work – though mischievous minds,
like mine, can't sort things out that way but dash
from *this to that*. It's hard to put a stop to such
indulgences. Intuitions tell us: *That to this*

is a sublime progression, even fooled about with
in our jokes on this and that. That we can raise
this tiny blaze from wispy literary gas
bestows a blissful glow on all our satisfactions.

Paintings, photographs

Paintings are not stopped by time.
You gaze into the eye of the face
upon a Roman coffin lid and wait
for it to blink. People skate

across a chilly Brueghel pond.
You watch as they begin to spin.
You know which one will fall.
The chair angled by Van Gogh

before his easel is pausing there
before he shoves it to one side
then strides towards the door.
Photographs can't capture this.

From those ancient, stock-still,
sepia portraits to the latest
thousandth-of-a-second action shots
of athletes, insects, birds

or babies crawling on a carpet,
what we witness is an instant
fixed forever by a clock – scenes
that stop dead in their tracks –

a fluid circumstance that seems
to have been frozen by a spell.
Paintings never aim to hold
such breathless power to arrest.

The first fiver

It was dark. My father locked the back door,
drew the curtains, then switched the light on.
He whispered, 'I've got something staggering
to show you. It's safe inside my pocket.

You may never see the likes of it again.'
Then he thought a little. 'I expect you will,
but not for donkeys' years to come.
It's the first I've ever owned in all my life.'

From his jacket he took a wallet, opened
its shiny leather mouth and triumphantly
plucked out a five-pound note. 'There,' he said.
'*A real bloody fiver* … A fiver. Look at it.'

I did so, then he actually let me touch it –
briefly, gently. His hands were shaking. 'A real
bloody fiver,' he gloated once again, before
he poked it back between the wallet's lips.

I'd had a glimpse of treasure and can't recall
when next I saw another dazzler like it.
It may have been a year or two. Then they
began to pop from pockets everywhere

and they became mere money. A while later
I saw a man bang down a roll of twenty fivers
on a table. They looked quite like a peeling,
old, infected, paper sausage. Mottled. Bloated.

You name it

We are getting along just fine.
The overpopulation of the planet
is heading for the stratosphere,
the weapons of mass extinction

now verge on the demented,
every day whole species are destroyed …
and what with waste, pollution,
corruption, global warming …

you name it … we are managing
our civilised, advanced techniques
with customary incompetence,
plus routine boasting, panicking

and unhinged recklessness.
And we can genuinely say that we
are either right or wrong, or often
in between, when selecting

worthwhile goals, or ignoring them,
or finding fatuous adventures
to inspire us, or not. You mightn't
read about it, yet that's the way

our technology is applied, or isn't.
And as this all takes place, or doesn't,
whimsy will support us dependably –
or, just as often, possibly.

Dreams, sentiments, inklings of belief
and spectacular delusions – all help us
flounder on as usual. We set
our lives by their availability,

and their most gratifying fix
is the joy of wishful thinking.
Pied Pipers play us flashy tunes
upon their flutes as we get led

down darkened streets to caverns
crowded with ecstatic wraiths
happy in the golden promise
that they have chosen to be free.

.

Top months for rhyme

This is the best day
there has been since
a great one I remember
which possibly could have been
sometime round about
November or December.

The sun is shining
and all the signs are that
it's going to blaze away
just like this all week
or it could last much longer still.
Perhaps till May.

It reminds me of a winter's night
some years ago. There was
a red-gold, fabulous full moon.
It lit our frozen skies
and melted frosty smiles in the
southern hemisphere's June.

That's it. Only March can summon
several parched and gasping
echoes of attractive rhymes,
then the calendar collapses
into April and July.
Burnt out, horrisonant times.

An email for today

for Janet

All things went well today,
though I admit that this was only
more or less and in a kind of
ultra-pretty-ordinary way.

There was a lawn to mow,
plus laundry, cleaning up
and then a bit of shopping –
with not much more to show

and no event to make me shout
or do a little dance;
time passed exactly in the way
days choose to drift about.

Yet I'd have liked to swing
in brilliant style to the corner
of the street, then take a bow
and clap my hands and sing.

And I'd have wished to feel
your presence in more than
just a distant dream –
love's reward is when it's real.

New Year's card, 2021

I've a pristine notebook
to begin the New Year.
Not a single word in it,
the pages are clear.

I've a brand-new eraser,
a pencil that's sharp –
and a tidy desk proves
I'm ready to start.

But it's hard to get going
and it's easy to guess:
poems feed off disorder
and need human mess.

Small catastrophes

Catastrophes arrive in two main sizes: vast
and unimportant. The large variety stuns us
with its cataclysmic horrors, the pocket-sized
comes coloured by a cloud of gas that leaks
from an eruption in our brains.

I faced a fine example of a slight catastrophe
just the other day when I tripped and dived
across a footpath so wide there was
no handy fence or hedge that I could grab
to help me break the fall. I bruised and lost

some bits of skin, plus all the air inside me,
so lay there prone and watched
two schoolgirls walk towards me talking
with a lot of animation, which gave me time
to fill my lungs again so I could offer them

an explanation of the sprawled position I was in.
To my astonishment they were not even
interested, but carried on as though they hadn't
seen me. They kept up a vivacious chatter
as they most delicately parted, one stepping

round me to the left, the other to the right,
but never looking down – and afterwards
they joined again and blathered on without
a glance behind. Glorious sangfroid …
I suppressed a groan of pain as I stood up again,

dusted off my grubby coat, checked
several bones and mopped up blood.
Of course, I should have been aware
that modern kids are educated to ignore
the deadbeats slumped in every street,

yet I managed to remember how, when young,
we had been warned to keep a wary eye
on freaks – which meant that we were told
to look. Catastrophes swell oddly
when you're breathless on the ground.

Old pal, with regrets and a hoary smile

i.m. Duncan McCormack, d. 25 January 2021, aged 88

Growing ancient slowly loosens a last grip on any sense
of dignity. I made a thoughtless quip that overstepped a line
which (many, many years ago) would not have needed
pointing out. It played on partialities that once were

clear enough to warn me to shut up – yet I followed this
with a remark of such befuddlement that it ankle-tapped me
as I turned and the next thing there I was, breathless
and spreadeagled, gazing upwards from the grass.

My oldest pal, of course, felt an entitlement to bad-mouth
all my defects as I staggered up again, for they also had him
in their clutch – we'd known each other for more than
eighty years, so add rich righteousness, plus several gins,

and we had ammunition for some effective choices
of targets to attack, even though few of them had substance
from the start. We weren't exactly witty, but I think
we did display a batty whimsicality and style – then next

my pal decided that his turn had come to overstep a line
with some unrelated, dippy comments on a hoary,
muddled matter of great damage he once caused. I knew
the story well and there was now no other option but to go.

A time would come to think about his words. It would not
be fun, but friends can find a sort-of resolution in calmer
afterthoughts. Then death stepped in and put an end to that.
It's too absurd, for now there's no more to be done.

On the road with Mike

i.m. Michael Illingworth

One chill evening Mike and I got stuck in Canterbury
while hitching to Dunedin. It was in the 1950s
and the night was coming on, so we were just about
to choose a cosy haystack or a hedge, when a Jaguar

screamed past at a hundred *miles* an hour – then
stopped and backed towards us at almost that same
clip. Two wool buyers sat in front and they were
taking time out from their high-paid jobs to attend

a party in Dunedin and invited us to come along
then we could doss down later on the floor. It was dark
and there was hardly any traffic, so we stuck to triple figures,
until we turned off for refreshments at a country pub

which hadn't heard of laws to close its doors at six.
Mike and I had very little cash, but the buyers ordered
top champagne, and wine and whisky, then just as it
came time to settle up the driver said, 'Let's play

a game of darts to see who pays the bill.' And Mike
emphatically yelled, 'Yes.' The buyers could throw well,
but Mike had real class and it was therefore just bad luck
when the last dart fell to me – for I was a dunce at darts.

Then a most extraordinary event took place. I had to hit
a double-2 to win, and it's a tiny strip of brilliant red
that kept on jigging round. So I closed one eye to keep it still
and magically that little, outlying scrap of 2 began to spread.

It ballooned as big as any barn we'd passed along
the road. No way could I miss it, even if I tried. It swelled
until 2 filled the pub. All I had to do was calmly aim
a dart in front of me – and in it went! A sensation,

a moment of pure Zen, a whizz, a prodigy! And the bill
turned out to be so huge it would've ruined us.
Often since I've called on this same energy for help.
It never answers me. Wonders turn up only once.

At the official dinner

One night he was invited to occupy the chair
right at the top of the table. He thought this was
an honour and was surprised to find he could not
hear the conversations as they prattled past him

on both sides. He sat in a vocal crossfire
and lost all track of what was being said,
aware that he was in full view yet utterly apart
and therefore here as an object on display,

not to be listened to. He found he had
to endure a celebration where the deference
he had expected cast him into total isolation
and all he was required to do sporadically

was nod his head agreeably to prove he wasn't
fast asleep. Then worse, he saw that no one there
was going to try even to use him for their
target practice. He imagined that this is what

people do when they think you've gone
completely rusty and believe you cannot duck
the arrows, dodge the blows or sidestep neatly
from a well aimed kick. They'd just suppose

that anyone could dust him up or take him down –
so there he sat, surrounded yet alone,
smiling darkly and frowning painfully
through the uproar of the dinner babble –

and it took an hour and several drinks before
he registered in panic that he had gone insane.
He explored this dangerous new awareness
by making weird remarks, but no one

took the slightest notice – so afterwards, at night,
in bed, he buried his head in piles of pillows
and practised the final skill that he retained:
honks, howls, shrieks and manic laughter.

Working things out

Poems can concern themselves with anything they like.
They're not obliged to be about momentous issues
or shake their fists ferociously from placards.
Sometimes poems really do strike moral attitudes,

fire off worthy judgments and assert themselves
with passion, truth and conscience – though
meaningful intentions can too easily end up as lines
of posturing and affectation. The trouble is that most

prescriptive poetry demands your unconditional
acceptance, then your commitment, and soon enough
this all leads on to little, hazardous and hidden extras,
including a necessity for you to shut your ears

and close your eyes to rolls of rotten writing.
A poem often works more subtly and effectively
when it's left to make up its own mind about why
it chooses sides, the attitudes it decides to throw

its weight behind and the good intentions it may wish
to question or promote. Usually a poem knows exactly
where it's heading. The words will find a personal pattern
they hanker to reveal – or sometimes to conceal.

KM, Wörishofen and 1909

1909 doesn't ring in the mind. It was a year
of far-off wars, uprisings and collapses.
Schoolkids may recall that Shackleton
set off for the South Pole and Taft became
President of the US, Diaghilev brought

the Russian Ballet to the West, while Bleriot
achieved the implausible by flying across
the English Channel. Oh, and by
an extraordinary conjunction of the stars,
a Mrs Bowden, now better known

as Katherine Mansfield, went to Wörishofen
in various kinds of far-fetched trouble,
the worst of which may now appear to be
that she was under the purse strings and control
of a Mrs Beauchamp, who was her mum

and there to take command and, by chance,
to cover up the mishap of a stillborn child.
Somehow, we accept all this, shake our heads,
then read KM's short fictions that record events
which all state perfect living truths.

The best we can do

It takes some real commitment
to go on writing poems, for it's not
the kind of task that pays the rent.
It has its share of pleasure, but if it were
a business you'd end up going bust.

My modest profits have mostly
vanished into books and casual cases
of good wine. They would never
have supported a mortgage or a loan,
though sometimes I may have

found a bottle I had overlooked.
My friends and I can never place ourselves
among the serious practitioners.
Consider Bethell, Brasch, Curnow,
Duggan – and note that's just a sample

and the order's alphabetical
and strictly gender-equal (so shrug
aside the Glovers, Fairburns, Baxters,
who wouldn't try to fit) …
What was I saying? Oh yes,

poetry should define and honour nation,
nature and high narratives of dreams;
top poets must be lofty, sage, obstinate
and mean every word they write;
plus, those were the good old …

Again, I've somehow lost the thread …
I think the point I hoped to make may well
have been that you can pick the mavericks
from the way they poke their tongues out,
especially in exalted company.

Upright, pensive, rigorous heavyweights
correctly rule the high poetic roosts.
The rest of us make out the only way
we can: we celebrate nonsensicalities,
absurdities, balls-ups, jests.

Bolts from the blue

We used to examine what we confidently thought
to be the workings of our suspect attitudes by lifting off
their fancy labels, checking out the features underneath,
testing their components, then looking for the patterns
we might find. The process wasn't all that rigorous,
but it led from the particular to the general.

Now we've speeded up our methods and they're
driven more by intuitions, bright ideas, suspicions.
'Bolts from the blue' is one of the more vivid phrases
that we use to gloss these snappy tactics to ourselves –
its short yet incandescent words endorse
an absolute commitment and vividly imply

a vigorous application, and are backed up by
the fireworks of such fabulous expressions as
keeping 'up to the mark' with 'broad horizons' that
reflect our 'highest aspirations' while we keep trickily
'in step with the spirit of our times'. Everyone agrees
that glitzy categories help illuminate our paths.

And since this more or less appears to seem
like progress, why should we need more evidence
that our generalities are heading in the right direction
with thoroughgoing confidence and copybook restraint?
Particularities can only cast a tiny, flickering shadow
on our radiant range of slick expressions.

Document1

The poem you are reading is called
Document1. My computer
slapped the name on it when I forgot
to give it one of mine.

Yet from this inattentive start
Document1 has served
quite as well as any other handle,
for the sole event it makes

an effort to record was:
I could in no way recollect
for several irritating minutes
(gazing from an upstairs window)

the old name of a common
small green bird
picking insects from a plum tree
in the garden. Straight away

I knew it was a waxeye,
but tauhou or the 'little stranger',
which we, as children,
were pleased to call it years ago,

came back to me only after coffee.
As I returned to writing,
then gazed distractedly again
from the aforesaid window,

a bird (possibly the selfsame one)
returned to what was irrefutably
an unchanged plum tree. That's all
the poem ever meant to say.

Nothing else took place. The bird
remains a little stranger
and the poem still stays
as Document1.

The poem that just floated off

As I was lying on my back in bed,
a fully finished poem glided from me.
Not the one I'm writing now,
but an earlier, much more stylish version.
It took off gently from my mind
as I was blinking in the morning sun.

It's distressing to remember how,
as I rose fast to find a pen and write
it down, the poem floated there, a minute,
then side-slipped through an open
window and I lost sight of it.
It simply melted into air.

'Standing upright here' is a recipe
for pure disaster. Lie out flat
at dawn and never make a sudden move.
Be stealthy – always keep a small net
close at hand to catch the dreamy poems
as they go swooping past.

Here comes the rain

The weatherman foretells that thunderstorms
are aimed at us and, as I gaze outside, a cloud of ink
already blots out whole hills with a dumb deliberation –
thick and lumbering, sluggish and without remorse.

A downpour soon will slash this baleful darkness
with claws of steel – and we shudder as we grasp
how it will go about crude savagery and give no thought
to punishment, reward or piety. It will pelt us

hard as nails. An age has passed since rain last
picked on us to prove its pride in grim indifference –
exactly that same lack of pity as when (so long ago)
it cleared off, ignoring those who shook their fists

in rage against the arid, blistering skies it left
and taking not the faintest scrap of notice of the prayers,
pledges or profanities we hurled upon the drought
this caused. We wasted gales of breath upon it.

The cracks that ripped our bare, burnt lawns seemed
here to stay. Some of us, with empty water tanks,
went off our heads with worries over baths –
and no one dared to leave a wayward garden hose

in sight. Yet now we must endure the likelihood
of floods. After the deluge I can only hope that we
are sure to keep our fingers crossed when next
we beg for scorching, blinding sunshine to return.

Beyondabilities

Some dreams are triumphs of crackpot theatre,
with visual effects and entrances and exits
far too batty, fluky or outrageous to be displayed
and framed on any stage or screen. So how dismal

and exhausting it was last night to have to watch
performances of trite and dreary melodrama.
I'd laboured nonstop through the day, then I'd toppled,
zonked out, into bed, and I was confident I'd earned

a front seat in the offbeat theatre of my brain –
expecting tricks and gags, big-budget nonsense,
brilliant impossibilities – and not to be fobbed off
on my pillow with a shabby offering of trash.

The mind should never shirk its duty to repay us
with some mad beyondabilities for our daily obligation
to handle humdrum acts like sweeping, cooking,
washing dishes, paying bills and going off to work.

Dark night of the soul

He walked into the deepest valley of the night and discovered
he could touch then stroke the texture of the dark.
Later, he defined its 'floaty softness' as 'the velvet hair
of cats', then thought a bit and added it was 'animate

yet full of dread'. But then, this fearful sensation was followed
by a catastrophic loss of speech, which was more than dumbness,
for he lost the power of definition – and he described it,
afterwards, as entering a 'violent, breathless emptiness',

like being 'knifed then gutted'. He seemed at first to pitch
and tumble, as if spinning in a void, yet he could somehow
also apprehend that this was contradicted by a monstrous,
shrouded force that 'shadowed' him in every blind, lost space –

filling him with terror far more absolute than the appalling hush
that had afflicted him when he had brushed the surfaces
of pitch-black emptiness, for it now began to issue
babbling resonances that had no relevance to implication,

purpose or any past experience, until finally he leant
in his despair against a blackness of complete unknowing
that stretched beyond the last, faint echo of his being.
This magic instant of a boundless nothingness was as if

he had been turned completely inside out, to be reborn –
then sudden certitudes of meaning energised his every breath
and words again spread crackling wings of fire, and nullity
was radiantly transformed into the living sky of dawn.

Inner meaning

It is an endless abstract business
sitting at a desk and trying to hit on faultless words
to describe a picture in your head. You are attempting
to translate complexities of shape and colour
into a concentrated code of letters.

Which is how I'm now caught up
in memories of the way this morning I paused
inside a neighbour's garden, where I was feeding a holiday
breakfast to her cat, and goggled at the way
it basked in Providence – though that's

a place I've never visited, a contradiction
that may lie in the different ways the cat and I
interpret and proceed upon some incidental evidence,
which (as I started off by saying) I later had
a shot at converting into written signs,

though the picture that I tried to render
into lines of words had just a loose connection
with cats, food, kismet and the time of day. What briefly
caught my eye was a tiny yellow blossom, dangling
from a shrub, shimmering with dew,

out-flashing even the early morning sun,
seeming, while it lasted, to be about to gloss itself
into a golden phrase. I'm glad I did not try to construe hidden
meanings, but I do lament that moment's passing –
and the loss of such spellbinding light.

Writer at work

Oblivious and alone, yet testing
his words out loud, sometimes for hours
on end, he sits on a creaking, wooden chair,
drinking tea and running wrinkled hands
distractedly through his unkempt, grey
and thinning hair.

From time to time a poem
dreams itself into his head and –
though this is never going to happen every day –
the result is often yet another brimming bin
of crumpled A4 paper to be bagged,
collected, thrown away.

For years he's known that making
human contact by this method has its limits,
especially when he finds he's tangled in a rhyme,
and it worries him that he's become a bad
example of the inefficient use
of hours of working time.

And yet the poems keep piling up
in spite of all these stricken thoughts –
in fact, they merely seem to aggravate his cares.
But the double factor keeping him at work
is that he has a room all to himself
and untold years to spare.

Happy tidings

I met a neighbour in the park. 'Celebrate
the best news in the world,' she said.
'It's high time something happy happened.'

She rushed away without another word,
so I shouted after her, 'I hope you dent
the ceiling with a fusillade of corks.'

Later, I listened to the radio, scoured the news
on my computer and switched on the TV,
but there was not one glimmer of a hint

of anything remarkable. I gave up, poured
a drink – then laughed. I had a neighbour
in a million. A total lack of headlines

was a providential glory to be treasured.
I put my feet up, chose a book, and basked
in blankness, non-events and peaceful pleasure.

Maps of life

The way ahead in life is clearly marked –
every pathway has been mapped in black
and white – and if it were not for the patches where
the ink has blurred or blotched, plus the many sections
totally obscured by signs that draw attention

to slips, collapses, washouts,
fractures and a hundred other hazards,
you could stride along with confidence upon
a trip that ought to be as easy as it is to fall asleep,
for it's over as you cross from birth to death.

Early on I studied several maps of life
and noticed that among their many quirks
they pointed in quite different directions yet always
ended at a matching spot – which helped me choose
to push along without a need to use one.

And since that destination never changes
and the same old obstacles remain in place,
a path will easily select itself without the slightest
need for guides. Besides, a mapless mind can gaze around
and concentrate entirely on the view.

Best cooked food day

Today is Poetry Day –
a once-a-year event that encourages me
to add it also took these South Sea islands the same
three-hundred-and-sixty-five-and-a-quarter days
to spin through space and greet
official summer yet again.

Just like Poetry Day
our summer turns up on our calendars
exactly as envisaged, even though it seems a haunted,
neverending interlude to those who treasure heat
and light – though, as ordeals go, that's quite
impossible to measure.

However, the one thing I've been
often guaranteed is that the wait for public
recitations does not endure nearly long enough for those
who find exquisite pain in demonstrations
of the collective psychic therapy
that such events propose.

Which brings to mind this person
who told me she would always celebrate
the anniversary of the finest Sunday dinner I had ever
cooked then served upon her kitchen table –
though unhappily, I must confess
that these days it is never

easy to be positively sure where
or when this splendid meal was put together
or if there was an independent witness – but in any case
those were the words I think she used, and I also have
some confidence (possibly confused
or entirely misplaced)

that I recall her verve,
the twinkle in her eyes and the moisture on her lips.
Today, again, is Poetry Day – which you may well find trying,
though just like most days in a year you may
reach out as you cross a street
and catch a poem flying.

Encirclements and arrows

'I've a hunch this has to be my final book
so why not celebrate?' I jotted down these words
this morning when I spread my papers right across
the desk and began to decode scribblings with more
encirclements and arrows than a childhood movie

of the Wild West. The thought of picking up a pen
to dot a full stop that would mark an end
to multi-decades of devotion, hit me with such
a soothing and delicious weariness that I had to
stretch out on a rug for half-an-hour to recover.

Imagine that you've served a lifetime sentence
for a crime you did not know you had committed,
then you snap and cast away your shackles –
and decide you'll never need to muse again
in stanzas calloused sometimes by a gungy rhyme.

Tonight I raised a glass to liberty – yet after that
the old fixations began to stray back through my mind.
I found a pen to scrawl, with all the usual arrows
and encirclements: 'Where's the purpose
when there's nothing left to write?'

Heading back by tram

Some days can make it really difficult
to keep things moving. You set off
to a distant suburb not visited in years,
then you get stuck at an intersection
where the street signs have gone missing.

Maybe you're lost. Or perhaps it's just that you
are momentarily confused as you become aware
of the morning sky's strange cast – or possibly
there is a baffling fragrance in the air.
No one can help you with these problems.
Passers-by turn out to be strangers to the district.
They also have no maps. They gaze at you
uneasily. You realise that you may be
infected by a fragrance or a cast.

If only we could sweep aside such days,
but their minutes keep rattling on like the ghosts
of tramcars that once jangled through this part of town.
Right into the evening you could tell precisely
where you were. Their rails – those infallible, iron,
arterial connections, fanning out from a single heart
at the very centre of the city – always guided you.
Now you shut your eyes and can't help swaying
as you recall reaching overhead to clutch
a looped handgrip dangling from a strap.

And that's never quite the end of it, for when you think
you've made it safely home, the front door shuts
with a triumphant clatter – the exact sound made
by the slamming, two-way, wooden backrests
of seats on Auckland trams. Once more you hear
the piercing clanging of a bell, the iron wheels shrieking
in their tracks. There's a dim amber light inside
and a sparking crackle overhead – and forever you recall
the bang and slap of seats at every terminus. Blind,
lurching phantoms still clank across my brain. They've lost
their destination signs. I'm forced to rub at steamy windows
as I strain to peer into the coming dark.

Peter Bland exposed

Sorry about this, Pete, but one day soon
the poetry authorities are going to lock you
in a cell and put you through a harrowing and possibly
unspeakable cross-questioning.

In that dank and hellish hole you're sure to find
you've got a lot of themes to answer for that you
either think you've got away with or you've never
let them cross your conscious and incautious mind –
for instance, how will you explain, through all the wax
and insect life and static that blocks the ears of those
in power over pure poetics, that one lunchtime
recently you read out loud your latest poem
to Bernard and myself – merely for a bit
of wicked pleasure – and we came
down with the infection? That's
exactly how we picked it up.

When we scuttled back by bus and ferry
to our various dens both of us discovered,
to our horror, that we had lost control – yet before
we understood what this condition meant, our hands
had picked up mindless ballpoint pens and we were writing
poetry without permission – entirely about
absurdities and frivolous events.

No excuses this time, Pete. You gave it to us.
The poem you brought was instantly contagious.
Bernard and I had come out only for the food and wine,
plus a genuine bit of fun and hardcase chat …
Nothing like poetry attracted us …

it was you who got us going. We had no idea
that odd and shameful acts of prosody could happen
in broad daylight, against all natural laws
and common sense. It wasn't us.
The blame's entirely yours.

Tottering to destiny

It was exhilarating to be told on the radio
today, that our recurring thoughts
can guide us happily and directly
to our destinies, for if we are controlled

by clockwork repetitions then it also makes
good sense to tidy up those careless times
when we were well aware that we
weren't thinking straight

and to clean up every fantasy and puzzle
with our nightmares. It's a buzz to know
that a compelling repetition hangs around
to reassure us when finally

we climb down, bone-tired from the saddles
of our dreams and catch our breath
by leaning on the streetlamps of our hopes.
It ought to fire us up to be informed

that what we think is what we shall become.
On the one hand it's an easy answer
to the problem of exactly where
we're tottering off to – and

on the other it so attractively replaces
trying to find a path to understanding
by amusing us with programmed destinies
and obvious desires.

Lazy Day on Earth

This is an idle poem. It took its own sweet time
to entice me from the comfort of my bed
on a freezing morning and do some feeble
breathing exercises (more like little yawns)

so that it might have just sufficient strength
to cling on to reality and even squeeze a drop
of good sense from the blunders, contradictions,
sad absurdities and the mad baloney

that get passed off to every living soul
as conclusive proof of human progress.
I fortified the poem with a breakfast of hot toast,
scrubbed it under a steaming shower,

and in return it hummed and hawed, then asked
for help to choose a shirt and jacket.
Poems use a stack of devious, polished tricks
and shortly afterwards I heard this prize example

ring a friend of mine and say it had a cheery
and inspiring hunch that we deserved another
Lazy Day on Earth. And next it took us out,
then made me pay for lunch.

The point of writing about writing

'No one in their right mind wants to know
any artful convoluted thing that writers ever write
about their writing' – or so I was told the other day.

And I thought, how dim and narrow can you get?
There's a hypnotic interest in the way a record's kept
of strange behaviour and obsessions. In fact,

I've always wished to read about the methods
used by those who feel devoted to and write about
things I gave up quickly or which I've never done

and never even dreamed of sampling for myself.
It's not so much that I would ever hope to crack
a curious craze or a compulsion, it's more a wish

to enter and examine an unexplored experience
through the wondrous labyrinths of someone else's
eyes, illuminated by the strategies of their reactions.

Writing, fishing, popping corks or walking in the hills –
they exhilarate me mostly when my remembrance
is a frame that hangs upon a choice of words.

Earthquakes change everything

It takes one hell of a bang to wake me up at three a.m.
and this one was a shocker. I felt angry at the way
the hotel was being run, for (like everybody else)
I had come here to enjoy a pleasant panorama of the hills
and valleys that flow down to a distant sea – and the sloshed

and staggering drunk, whom I supposed had roused me
from a blackout sleep when he had flung his body
at my landscape-gorging, floor-to-ceiling window,
must have come extremely close to smashing his way in.

But over breakfast word went round that the culprit
was in fact a vicious, little earthquake – one that the hotel
had been designed impressively to absorb, though
nothing could be done about the startling sound effects.
What next impressed me even more was how the talk

among the guests so swiftly changed from actual tremors
to general reappraisals of the view. Overnight the scenery
had withered. A woman said it looked as though the hills
weren't trying hard enough. Some had shrunk or slumped

and no longer matched the glossy pictures in the brochures.
A main fault was their dismal green. Why not reds and golds?
An old man mentioned that the clouds, which only yesterday
had all the solid puff of cauliflowers, now seemed limp
and stained and soggy – then he joked that the hotel staff

should peg the sky out on a line and give it a good airing.
All agreed that it was getting cold, with a likelihood of rain,
and we'd be wise to leave that day. The place had not lived up
to expectations. Not one more word was said about the jolt.

Old military families

All families have a military connection,
some a bit more professional than others,
but it's always present and correct. Like it or not,
plain survival has often enough depended
on it, whatever conscience or opinion may have
since decided. Both sides of my lot

have seldom talked about it, but it's there.
One great-grandfather was the colonel
of an Irish regiment, a grand-uncle's name
glows in letters of gold inside the dome
of the Auckland War Memorial Museum
for his involvement in the Boer War.

I'm a direct descendant of a man who fought
'with Nelson' at Trafalgar. Close or distant,
my relatives went where they were told to go,
whereas I've had the great good fortune
to choose issues I've supported or opposed.
I'm old and tired of it all, and now

feel only the greatest love and respect
for the regiments of them. Whatever they got up to
and wherever they went, they were people
of their times. I can't impose a distant right
or wrong on them, for history does that job
with its sure inconstancies. It's a cruel record

not so much for what it tells us of the things
we did, or failed to do, but for the changing ways
we read it. The past has altered so much
since I was a boy that it cannot help but seem
a dangerous place. Best to go there unafraid
and choose to face the ancestors of us all.

Problems with images

The central image of a poem
I read by chance, described a river's 'scales'
glistening in the sun as it 'snaked' along a looping
valley floor – 'sliding, slithering' past the limestone bluffs
and ridges of surroundings that I know quite well.
There was no enchanting, wild hyperbole.
It just made free with facts.

Lizards, grey worms, whitebait, eels,
North Auckland worms, nightcrawlers –
any of them may have worked okay, but our only
snakes spend their entire lives at sea, and as far as I know
neighbouring land-snakes live two thousand
kilometres west. There are no snakes
in any valley here. Not one.

Some would say that lots of us have met
Serpentes on our travels, and almost everyone
must have heard of them or watched them writhing
over screens, so eventually I had to tell myself that poets
have a right to dream them into curving dips
in landscapes where they've
actually never been.

Incongruity lies at the heart of poetry.
Words in verse so often can suggest a kind of
double-take on what we think we've seen – and aim
to open up our minds to the uncustomary. I read the poem
once again and the river made it this time, painfully,
to sea. It wriggled past me in the end.
Twisting. Twitching. Squirming.

Old age and optimism

It's not the shortness of your breath that tells
your friends and family you no longer measure up –
the give-away is the muddle you get into.
A doddering brain clicks into neutral when

the pressure's on. Your reactions need to rest
before they're ready. Trembling hands may still
pour tea and wobbly legs may steer you to a chair,
and sometimes you may socially scrape by

with half-remembered anecdotes from somewhere
in your foggy past, but it takes an age before
your brain can switch on in a crisis. And it takes
another age before you are aware you've got away

with it again. But what good luck it is to have
a disability with such optimistic outcomes.
So far, others step in smartly to retrieve the situation,
so why it worries them is a mystery indeed.

A Valentine's Day card

As the years twist on
and the months form vines
and the days entangle
and their minutes entwine
will you thread, then bind,
my Valentines?

Explaining to the waiter

What you intend to set down when you start a poem
doesn't always end up in the lines you write,
just as sometimes when you talk the sounds get chewed
and people think you've uttered sentences you'd never
dream of. They must imagine thoughts are mad enough
to jump off from your tongue. And days are quite

the same, in spite of having perfectly distinctive
names and numbers as they line up on a calendar.
This morning, for example, as I got up from my bed,
did I spare one concentrated thought to identify
their accurate position in this orderly parade?
Did I take care to discover where 'tomorrow' stands

in the correct and unambiguous record of our times?
The answer is, of course I didn't. I thought tomorrow
is today, so now I'm eating here alone, explaining
to the smirking waiter, who's just served me food
and wine, that I'm only here for practice: 'Every stomach
needs good training. Mine's on a trial run.'

Rapture

All people that on earth do dwell
can't help but notice how the clocks
are speeding up and there's not a solitary second
left to waste – yet I find I cannot care about
the way time scurries past.

I gaze from windows and discover
pleasure in a bird, a cloud, a patch of open sea,
a smudgy island – and cannot force this poem to its end.
Words can take as much time as they please.
There's never need for haste.

An odd line from a hymn or song
goes drifting by with echoes of a time or place
that seem summoned by the breeze. And it is rapture
just to stand here in your love and listen –
apprehending, filled with grace.

Words out hunting

At any time of day there's writing going on,
the kind that's called creative (a label that
we oldies are suspicious of, and much happier
to apply to the dodgy aspects of accountancy).

Morning seems to be a favourite time when words
'creatively' hunt out jobs in serious books
or novels, essays, stories, other works. They often
show up in loud running gear, though many

slouch along in rags, and most appear to look
in set directions, sometimes stopping for a spell,
or drink, or just to pass the time by slouching in
the shade. Words that hunt for places in a poem

don't get about like that. They favour shortcuts
that will make a journey longer or get tangled
in a barbed-wire fence or vanish in the dark.
I've heard them rustle through dense undergrowth

while startled birds fly screaming through the trees.
Young poets have the energy to cope with all such
endless foraging. They'll rise from bed at dawn,
then wander far and wide in thought.

Uncannily, precisely, they can always spot
the latest phrases, take aim, then breathlessly
they'll bring them down. Hunters hunting hunters.
We oldies get along by gathering up the feathers.

The bad manners of speaking

A tortured listener called our local radio
to complain that many years ago she'd given up
tuning in because of the continual mispronunciation
of sublimely simple words – but today she hoped
this may have changed so she'd allowed it one last chance.
Sadly, it made her wince to have to send in this report:
No progress has been made.

Within a mere ten minutes, over the same airwaves,
I noticed how *co*-op-eration was being clipped short
into *cop*-eration, a *kilo*metre was deliberately stretched
a longer distance into kil-*om*-etre, no*th*ing ended up
as nu*ff*ing like it, and a f*i*sh became a f*u*sh – but I revelled
in this evidence that our language is alive
and full of error, bedevilment and energy.

Good rules should attempt to make a meaning clear
not teach a sour correctness that would also love
to shave our heads and straighten up our backs.
At school I can recall the comic cheek
of split infinitives, the fun of winking at subjunctives.
Our radio tries to get its tongue around the truth.
Up the genu-*wine* cham-*peens* of disrespectful speech!

Shouting back

The youthful thing to do about the rotten kind
of day that somehow you discover
you have landed in is to shake your fists
and shout abuse and curses at the elements.

Now and again a storm will turn up
out of nowhere and encourage you to stop
what you are doing and protest till you leave
no doubt that this time you have had enough.

I'd always thought that being forced
to suffer weather agony is compensated only
by an equal right to bellow back at it.
But I'm not so sure this morning.

The slumping firmament I'm gazing at
is hardly worth the fuss of a reply. And so
my fists relax. I peer into a grey and flagging
waste and can't sustain that old-time rage –

a slow and steady drizzle mopes about the hills,
clouds skulk by with a bizarre banality. Perhaps
I'll fold these lines into a paper dart, then shut
one eye and fire it point-blank at the sky.

The strange meaning of whatever

My life has amounted to a lightning visit to a place
we call The Earth. It floats around a star in a minor galaxy
in which there possibly could be another thirty or forty planets

inhabited, just like us, by malcontents and misanthropes
so distracted by the comic brevity of existence that in between
the satisfaction of their various urges they may in time
be vaguely interested enough to try to get in touch.

But don't depend on it. We spend our lives pursuing goals
that won't amount to very much. Death comes to all
and knocks us off – the same as monkeys, molluscs, microbes –

and we don't leave that many cherished records to distil
our wonder-moments, which may leave behind some simple sense
of goodness shared. Yet little that we do adds up to more
than dreams or love or the pledging of our passing beings

to the bliss and the excitement of the wild, stupendous triumphs
that occur in spite of many botches as we attempt to share
our joys, endeavours and ideals … until, perhaps, we have

the luck one day to learn that sadness can be nothing other
than a brooding, turning-back of time – then comprehend
that from this follows a discovery that we may draw
enchanted sweetness from every passing, fleeting second.

Cackling to ourselves

As you float slowly to the far end of the pond you lose
a lifetime's airy confidence that your old buoyancy
will keep on bearing you along. It takes years of effort
and endurance to cast adrift from the protective shallows

and set off for the tantalising deeps, only to discover,
after so much application, that they exist to try to suck
you down. However, the one great compensation is you get
to share the loony company of other ancient coots

whose fate it also is to tread these baffling waters –
without any of us ever being warned about the pain
of keeping going or how we'd one day learn that we've
been whispered to be drongos, freaks and clowns.

We oldies cackle to ourselves about the public platitudes
the young slop down upon us, the tricky, winking,
nudging yarns of how stout-spirited we were to launch
ourselves on our halfwitted and unfathomable adventures.

Yet it never causes us alarm. It's just a case of one more
wanton weaknesses we can turn into a joke.
Our single worry is that one of us may laugh too long
and loud, creating waves that any time could drown us.

Socks

Each morning, just before I rise, I'm delighted to observe
that the world has managed to survive another night
as it goes about its business of orbiting through space –

an achievement that has never been as simple as it sounds
for occasionally Earth has taken hits from flying objects,
on top of which these days it has to face a legion

of crazy saboteurs who'd love to blow it all to bits.
And when I've checked out that the globe is still intact,
I'm sorry but its problems then must take a second place

to the intricate, exhausting task of pulling on my socks.
I have found that routine cleansing duties – such as showers,
shaving, teeth – can occupy a lot of extra time and care

as we grow old, but socks are something else. It used to be
the case that I never had to spare my feet a thought.
They ran and skipped and danced about all day at the far end

of forgetfulness. Now they have become a constant nightmare.
To roll on socks and squeeze unwilling flesh into a shoe
requires strategy, determination, ingenuity and skill.

And after all that stress you then must consciously direct
your lower limbs to shuffle down a street. The young
have no idea of the gruelling, stumbling way ahead, or how,

when waking up and sparing first thoughts to the welfare
of the planet, these will soon seem pure indulgence as you
grit your teeth once more and battle with your socks.

Just like that

for Karl Stead

Karl, another poem
was sent to me direct
this morning.

Just like that.

It flew into the kitchen
completely out of nowhere.

One minute I remember
making coffee and the next
I must have blinked
or clicked my fingers,
then I looked up and saw
a mint-condition poem had arrived –
and it was tipping me the wink.

Talk about astonished –
I felt I had been knocked for six,
I was flabbergasted, freaked,
stunned, gobsmacked,
totally blown away.

Three very simple things happened
strictly in this sequence:
Coffee … Click … A poem …
Oh, plus of course,
there was that wink –
whatever it could possibly
have meant.

You never get accustomed
to how or when a poem will fly in –
just as, in a far more humdrum
and exhausting way,
you can't get used
to waving them goodbye
as sometimes they take wing again
and glide off to the setting sun.

Kevin Ireland | Shape of the Heart

Available from all good booksellers